Also by Shannon Webb-Campbell:

Still No Word
I Am A Body of Land

LUNAR TIDES

SHANNON WEBB-CAMPBELL

Book*hug Press
Toronto 2022

Cover artwork: *Lessons in Cyclical Growth* by Amy Ash,
cyanotype on dyed cotton, 43" (2021). Used with permission of the artist.

Library and Archives Canada Cataloguing in Publication

Title: Lunar tides / Shannon Webb-Campbell.
Names: Webb-Campbell, Shannon, 1983- author.
Description: Poems.
Identifiers: Canadiana (print) 20210372524 | Canadiana (ebook) 20210372532
ISBN 9781771667388 (softcover)
ISBN 9781771667395 (EPUB)
ISBN 9781771667401 (PDF)
Classification: LCC PS8645.E225 L86 2022 | DDC C811/.6—dc23

The production of this book was made possible through the generous assistance of the Canada Council
for the Arts and the Ontario Arts Council. Book*hug Press also acknowledges the support of the Government
of Canada through the Canada Book Fund and the Government of Ontario through the Ontario Book Publishing
Tax Credit and the Ontario Book Fund.

Canada Council **Conseil des Arts**
for the Arts **du Canada**

ONTARIO ARTS COUNCIL
CONSEIL DES ARTS DE L'ONTARIO
an Ontario government agency
un organisme du gouvernement de l'Ontario

Funded by the   Financé par le
Government   gouvernement
of Canada   du Canada

Canadä

ONTARIO | **ONTARIO**
CREATES | **CRÉATIF**

Book*hug Press acknowledges that the land on which we operate is the traditional territory of many nations,
including the Mississaugas of the Credit, the Anishnabeg, the Chippewa, the Haudenosaunee,
and the Wendat peoples. We recognize the enduring presence of many diverse First Nations, Inuit,
and Métis peoples and are grateful for the opportunity to meet, work, and learn on this territory.

For my moonshadow, my mother,
Diane (née Beattie) Campbell
(1959–2019)

losing: *Phrase losing of the moon;* the period of waning.
—*Dictionary of Newfoundland English*

I feel perfectly at home underwater.
—Anne Carson

Mama = your first ocean.
—Leanne Betasamosake Simpson

Remember the moon, know who she is. Remember the sun's birth at dawn, that is the strongest point of time. Remember sundown and that giving away to night. Remember your birth; how your mother struggled to give you form and breath. You are evidence of her life, and her mother's, and hers. Remember your father. He's your life, also.

—Joy Harjo

MOON PHASES

NEW MOON

WAXING CRESCENT

◗

FIRST QUARTER

●

WAXING GIBBOUS

FULL MOON

WANING GIBBOUS

LAST QUARTER

WANING CRESCENT

What phase was the moon when she left?

How high or low were the tides?

Spring tide: Sun and Moon at opposite sides (180°)

Neap tide: Sun and Moon at 270°

Spring tide: Sun and Moon at the same side (cycle restarts)

NEW MOON

TIME: A BIOGRAPHY

*A poet is Atlantic and lion in one. While one drowns us the other
gnaws us. If we survive the teeth, we succumb to the waves.*

—Virginia Woolf

I: Beginning

A baby is born in a room to a body. Hears her mother's voice. The baby wants to
return to womb waters. What is this room? What is this body? Living is a stretch.
Doctors assign sex. Only hours until you hear tides. Nothing prepares you for life.
Born three months premature. Are the grandmothers in my body? Doctors don't
like to answer these questions. Life becomes a quest of origin. Mother reminds us
why light thins. Passing into night, you return somewhere like wind.

A room. Body. Baby.

II: Beginning/Middle

In the room, in my body, mother tells the story of breath. Falling out of her one afternoon, nearly an entire season too early. The nurses pushed plastic tubes up my nose, put me in a glass box. Was she in the room? Was I once in *her* body? Birth explodes a new kind of meaning. Nothing prepared my mother to mother. Sex assigned her body. The hospital staff told her to go on home. I needed to keep breathing. Nurses took me away, and she was left to imagine holding her baby. Grandmother was islanded in time—thousands of miles away.

A room. A body. Waves.

III: End

Grief takes up with body. Mother never peed in front of me. Illness yellowed her, and took her socks. Palliative care is a tenth-floor view with an aluminum garden overlooking the city. Called in the middle of the night to be with her. Kin piled in cars, drove downtown, followed highway lines. A woman who wanted us there when she stopped breathing. A mother whose body never felt at home. Death exhausts in spectacle. Nothing prepared us for our last morning together. Was I in in the room? Was she in her body? I sat in the hospital window while her tiny sixty-year-old body slept. I couldn't take my eyes off her chest. Watching her laboured breath become a final hour. *It's okay to go*. I imagined a baby cradled in my arms, the way she once held me. Passing my baby to her, I cried oceans over them. This is the closest I get to giving her a grandchild.

The room. The body. Mother.

LIVING AT LOW TIDE

we come from different territory
our language is touch
until I lick the soles of your feet
after you walk the ocean floor

ECOLOGY OF BEING

in this thinner air
there is no need to *ingest crystals*
we are surrounded by the boreal forest
at the breakdown of natural order
within the great chain of chaos

we exist as intervention
between land and sky
only to return from a journey
to a place of familiarization

forgo the power of selfhood
pain is singular—
it triggers memorable experiences
if you embody new occult poetics

between the self and this other thing
we make a clearing to find meaning
travel to trembling aspens
and come upon medicines

we remember this leaf
make connections
experience seasons at their breaking point
and reinvent our skin cells

TIDES

are whales deep thinkers?
ask the tides that chart the rise and fall
on August's fullest lunar night
when the fish are jumping and
your moon's bleeding

tell me the answer at high tide
I'll ask you again at low tide
six hours and 13 minutes later
to see if you mean it

come back to the same spot
ask the moon what day it is
work 24 hours and 52 minutes into
a tidal rhythm

tell me about the whale carcass
whose rotting body has washed to shore,
harbour locals walking around
holding their noses

circle back, and plant some cedar
it takes a village to dispose of a dead whale
their bones shipped away to a museum

tell me the question at high tide
I'll answer again at low tide
six hours and 13 minutes later
to see if you remember

if whales are deep thinkers, do they know
it takes one day and 52 minutes for a point
on earth to be noticed
by the moon?

humans believe logic is time

we're all shift workers

here on the lip of Atlantic

DEFINITION

grief

/grēf/

>un: **grief**
>
>1. Sharp sorrows deepen during spring tides, especially those caused by the sun and moon on the opposite side.
>
>2. Deep sorrow, especially that caused by someone's death.

a very sad feeling, especially when somebody dies

- *She was overcome with grief when her mother died*
- *They were able to share in the neap tide of joy and grief*
- **grief for somebody/something** *her grief for her dead mother*
- **grief over something** *grief over the loss of mother*
- **grief at something** *She could not hide her grief at the death of life as she once knew it*

noun

Keen mental suffering or distress over affliction or loss; sharp sorrow; painful regret.

a cause or occasion of keen distress or sadness.

IDIOMS

come to grief *(informal)*

1. to end in total failure
All her plans for moving forward
came to grief.
2. to be harmed in an accident
Her son and daughter came to grief
in the hospital, and months, seasons,
years after.

give somebody grief (about/over something)

1. *(informal)* to be annoyed with somebody
and criticize their behaviour
good grief!
(informal) used to express surprise or shock
Good grief! I miss my Mom!

WHO AM I IN RELATION TO THE MOON?

earthworms contemplate horoscopes
a navigation tool across earth

lunar logic burdened by astrology
a missive turns eternal, you see a light
on your knees praying to the night

I am not moon
I am womb
I am moon
I am not womb

from this altar of various attempts
reposition celestial sky bodies
even small motions make the moon howl

BLOODSTONE NEW MOON

there's a childlike angry voice
boiling up and over chaotic
like agitated water yelling
if it's not mother's love, I don't want it!

you leave your body
to live above, a safer place
breathwork guides—a way to tell if
you're breathing into your jaw muscles
body scans bring your breath down
your rib cage bellies and expands

bring your knees up to source flow
blood nourishes your feet
Earth energy shoots through your body
your inner garden hydrates
vines grow stronger to your mother
shoulder blades sprout—
her small angel's wing

your reproductive organs want
to speak about being so serious:
release blockages, jump a few times
muscle spasms make pops
all breaths keep new flow going—
birth a feverish future

SUDDENLY AWARE (A LUNAR CYCLE BEGINS)

imagination reaches far
back into being—
of course, you're afraid
you are a skewed universe
learning to lean forward

WAXING CRESCENT

CODFISH

I recall mother whispering
before the womb,
asking me to fill her

on the stove
salt-back
pork pops in the pan, sizzles

almost tall enough to touch plaster,
I was lifted by Poppy's arms,
propped up by his big fish belly

my grandmother's catch of the day
makes her hum words
I don't understand but want to curl into

GREATER THAN AVERAGE TIDES

I think it's okay to be a little superficial
if you know you're trying to be Oceanus
or have life plans to map the moon

together you raise all the rivers
fountains overflow
lakes flood sex
your only way back

HOME WAS CALLING

hunters know elbow-deep
on the land we heal
surrounded by islands
pure smelts, wild earth
millions of yellow chanterelles

we're taught all mushrooms are poison
everything exists under a shadow
doubt is our limitation
our hearts lack belief

give Islanders courage
give us confidence
holding on to this place, its mosses,
roots and fossils
against all odds, we thrived

NEVER BEEN TO LABRADOR

I've never been to the *place where the current makes clouds*
I know my family lived there before I was born
my grandfather was a foreman on Churchill Falls
a hydroelectric project cutting off
cascades of water, once a powerful flow
now only a small stream trickles down its bed

we don't talk about Indigenous names
the labyrinth of environmental damage
settler's debts or what poisons Muskrat
he only recalls a company town

I wear labradorite on my middle finger
dream of iridescent rings lowering blood pressure
silvering clouds offering protection
balancing my moon's tension

I've never been to Patshishetshuanau
the *place where the current makes clouds*

OUR LITTLE GIRL'S BOOK

a soft pink look book of firsts –
a silver spoon, jumpsuit, shasta daisies
my first word: *Mum,*
both pink and yellow bunny suits,
Royal Doulton china, gold bracelet,
night light, christening dress, and
that bible from Aunt Vera

no gifts from my paternal kin,
save for Mi'kmaq blood, something no one
wrote down. I'm not sure who gifted
a small knit hat that barely holds my fist now

Mother, may I?
I can't ask you why.
Father, may I?
Now I know why you sigh.

record states: Reverend blessed this baby
despite an incomplete family tree,
recognized offshoots to maternal
great-grandmothers and grandfathers,
while father's branches were left blank

AURORA ALERT

I try to love mountainlike
surrounding and still
but I can't

you won't let me cover you
like aurora borealis
shaking the sky

you deflect solar flares
move like wind
or an opera

I want to mouth
your entire root system
but you are too afraid

you smell of pine
breathe soft timbre
drip like sap

I rub up against
your magnetic poles
to grow the moon

I TOLD YOU I DON'T BELIEVE IN SOUL MATES

only to find us folded
together like pages of a book
as if we were bound
by something other than life

EAST VERSUS WEST

before leaving, I kissed a mouth,
held a baby, and boarded a plane
to see light parade over Iceland

I woke up in Dublin,
where immigration glared at my passport
and asked what I did for a living

the Irish officer congratulated me
on being a poet—
you must return, *River Shannon*

I got lost several times today,
yet at every direction is a person
who reminds me there could be

a fella to love, a baby to kiss
if only I give up airplanes elsewhere

A WINTER SKY

under a feathering of stars
Orion pulls you from yourself
look upward to turn inward
greet the ancestors

tend to the cooking fires
let your love crackle
drink in existence
open your lover's mouth
together you gaze at the winter sky

SLEEPING WITH THE NORTHERN LIGHTS

I dream of drinking moon blood
my head next to Sleeping Buffalo
where wild light comes in in the dark

I wake to snow-dusted trees
on enormous glacial rock
breathe in dry oxygen

you are wilderness
I know you wished for me
long before I came into your womb

as you birthed us into being
another story surfaced

Mother, I will carry this wilderness forward

RISING TIDES

a fog engulfs the city, swallowing rocks,
until buildings disappear, traffic softens
you lose yourself in tidal time,
whatever gets you through

moonlit pinnacles edge waves
unifying rhythms of longing
a shadowy future of plain sand
a moment determined by touch

dark cave thieves—
we become the sea itself
shifting, grounding,
rising into a new shoreline

FIRST QUARTER

IF I WASN'T A FURY

I would know where I come from
I wouldn't believe my bones
were made of shit and shame

I could walk the land
speak with ancestors
know what to carry forward

but I don't know which plants
are good medicines
or how to braid sweetgrass

I can't speak my language
hold a drum or sing myself home
without crying

if I wasn't a fury
I would know where I come from

LONG DISTANCE CALL AT LOST LAKE

we seek the peace of broken ground
                              —Dorothy Livesay

walking an old-growth forest
under a marquee of pine, western hemlock
red cedar, Douglas fir, Whistler spruce
I smell earth awaken

we meet across time –
whispering as snow dusts mountains
finding one another on unfamiliar trails
you feel trees tip

our voices linger over Lost Lake
reminding us of what
we can no longer live without

this you, this me
everywhere

HINGE

a morning issued calm
like the flap of a wave
until chill and sharp
                   some internal ailment

the rooks rising, falling
his eyes stiffened
waiting for a touch of light
since her illness

how many years now?
waking at night, a particular hush,
the hour, irrevocable
grey-blue morning air

strange high singing
thank Heaven
it was still so early, a stirring of mesh

whirling errands of old sea green
absurd and faithful
kindle and illuminate
her silence

MOON AND SUN REINFORCE ONE ANOTHER

synchronicity summons land and water,
all feral creatures know this

if we are almost free underwater,
why does body require
life on land?

we're all dying out here
treading water in our own way

SOLAR POISON

I've been making out with the sun
I can no longer kiss you with these sunburnt lips
a mouth too hot
a tongue too slow
my bottom lip blister swells

A VARIATION ON ALCHEMY

Light candles, burn sage,
welcome spirits. Humbled devils mingle,
drinking thin moonlight on a Laurier terrace.

Mischief and magic meet at this party,
where we down night wisdom, offer up
wonder to our inner mappings.

Lilacs downwind ask for guidance.
Ancients laugh it off, dancing into our cups.

SEA CHANGE

if whales have everlasting memory
then what does the moon recall?
some say grandmother

I've followed whales from Saint Andrew's
all the way down to K'taqmkuk's south shore
saw a breach off Mistaken Point,
where minkes greeted the Bell Island ferry
some nudged Witless Bay boats

I've seen ex-lovers, whale ancestors
when a sperm blows, you'll know kinship
intimacy lives underwater
connects us to other realms

SHE LOOKS STRAIGHT AHEAD

on my last night in the Plateau a sultry bartender
dances atop the table with another femme,
champagne coupes popped, arms raised
under half a dozen stuffed ostrich heads came back to life:
mouths agape, eyes wide, necks swinging left to right
as the dancer harnesses girls from Ipanema
who sashay and go *ahhh*
leaving this city in spring was a particular kind of woe—
now we're all missing Montreal

LUNAR VIBRATIONS

opening into different dimensions
no longer bound by outworn metaphysics
moving towards a field, all that's non-local

an instinct arrives
activates the solar plexus
golden gifts appear
bringing perspicacity
a revolution

death—another frequency
restructuring perception
cleansing consciousness
fully releasing cosmic tensions
committing your etheric body towards
a collective capricious lover

WAXING GIBBOUS

I AM PULSAR

I am burning
a white dwarf developing
a star coming into being
I was born billions of years ago
came through the grandmothers

I am a lonely heavenly body
on a light path unknown to itself
before I was a star I was dust
always in flux
I spin and spin and spin
then I disappear
sometimes I go dark

even though I'm light years away
I still exist in gravitational waves
it took me billions of years to become this star

I used to think I was a star from the suburbs
turns out I'm older than time
a star born through giant red
a mother's light

I thought I was an average star
turns out I'm at the end
light expelling its outer material
creating planetary nebula
becoming hot core remains

I am a disappearing star
only visible to those
who can see light dim

I am becoming the dust of stars
once a star of the land
named after a quasar
one of the many lights
who don't belong in a black hole

I am a dense star
a star older than time

CENTRELINE

our lives take us down
unmarked roads, grocery store aisles,
along borders, through time

we are small against tides

we must leave this all
better than when we got born

SHORT TALK FROM ITALY

of all the worldly wonders
nothing quite thrills me
like the stationary horses
on that carousel in Florence

POEM FOR A PHANTOM VALENTINE

Every Feb. 14, the bandit puts up paper hearts
and heart banners all over the city.
It's a tradition that dates back to 1976.
                    —Kathleen Jordan

if someone mistook me for a Valentine's Bandit
I'd stay up all night postering Portland with paper hearts
banner a small flurry of sleepless Cupids
all over a city built around a port
coaxing building owners to hand over keys
and hold on to our secret—
unrequited love inhibits movement

ROOFTOP ORACLES

Oracle I

East brings prophetic predictions
Northern Oracle's massive wooden housetop
spans light's architecture

Oracle II

North explores physical space points to
abstract thinking, opening us to possibilities
and a rekindled relationship to Africville

Oracle III

West interrogates
reconsiders lost
and hidden histories,
how race reshapes land

Oracle IIII

South climbs the roof to reposition ideas of power,
looks through a peephole: the artist invites you
to press gold into the drawing in exchange for a wish

LIMINALITY

in the incubator
a sense of enclosure
breathing in what comes next
opening to what spirit wants

once out of the box
start sitting on curbs
remember how to lie
learning how to run

wish I could knock on all the doors
of my childhood friend's homes
show them how tall the trees are

POSTSCRIPTS & MOON TEA

a cacophony of children's voices pass by my window
walking hand in hand, singing out to the day
while the light catches selenite streams
made of water, wind, sand

this morning marks a thousand crossroads
sorting through boxes of letters and photographs
old pockets of intimacy and memories
I find my grandmother's handwriting
on the back of a bank statement

rereading the last line, I ache for her
whether near or far, I have loved you every moment of your life
get choked up at her postscript projection:
so please be careful, don't walk around the city at night,
unless selenite glistens and *you are with someone*

Poppy phones to share last night's dinner
a salmon burger cut in half after a double Scotch
what he calls *the good life*

I come across a black-and-white photo
of a young fella in Verdun wearing an oversized suit
Poppy coughs, and says *that's me at ten in 1944*
remembers wearing his adopted father's jacket
because his boy arms were too long

I find another opal Post-it Note with instructions
charting my grandparent's intricacies
Poppy clears his throat chakra, and listens

Bob, don't throw out my tea

KEPE'KEK / AT THE NARROWS

who lived at the mouth of Turtle Grove
when disruptions came in boats across grey coast?
Mi'kmaq relations settled on these lands and waters
families called this home Mi'kma'ki
lived in wigwams, weathering climate and settlers
whites claimed land to build flats on Hollis Street
Mi'kmaq asked government to relocate to Albro Lake
three years and counting, the community ready to go
a week before transatlantic toxic boats
blasted into fire, exploding Kjipuktuk

FULL MOON

OUR COVE HOUSE

I'm thinking of our bodies
how I came from your womb
and my body took over your being

I'm remembering
how stressed you were by my need for milk
you were starved for something else

I don't know if I could mother
feed mouths who didn't want to eat dairy
or don't want to be here
arguing over if they want to live

our old cove womb
its sunken-in floor, wood stove kitchen
narrow staircase up to four bedrooms

an archive of what can't be bought
from a fisherman twenty years ago
whose daughters didn't want to see it go

PORTALS

1. everything supposedly exists in opposition—pivots against intuition
2. polarities inhabit a body that seeks unity
3. centre your feet to remember something we used to know how to do
4. geometric patterns form in sand, water, oil to create spirals found in the liver
5. industry smashes against nature
6. colourful sounds fuse bone
7. transformation is the crux of death

GRIEF: Q&A I

Q: How does grief feel?

A: I'm at the bottom of the ocean, screaming below water, looking up to pearl-grey eyes.

Q: How do you cope?

A: I circle shops we used to go, towns we once visited, I even went to down the southern shore. I can't find her, keep asking strangers—*have you seen my mother?*

Q: What am I doing here?

A: Part of me isn't here. Part of me is elsewhere with her.

Q: How can I go on without her? Why isn't my mother here?

A: I try to remember she gave me this life, and try not to waste it.

Q: What did your mother teach you?

A: She never taught me how to live without her.

GRIEF: Q&A II

Q: What are the five stages of grief?

A: Denial, anger, bargaining, depression, acceptance.

Q: Do you think there are more stages?

A: Yes.

Q: Like what?

A: Ask the displaced moon.

MENAGOESG REDUX

Wolastoqiyik and Mi'kmaq peoples
living with lands and waters
Menagoesg

this place was breathing long before
de Monts and Champlain sailed
or Loyalists washed ashore

after gumboots walked the ocean floor
or taste buds craved purple dulse
seeking a bay of old-world architecture

a windy place, we call it
now fading paint-stained buildings
a wild where nature meets industry

we gave up colonial hours
clocks returning internal
rhythms to tide tables

others note moons cycling
ancient burial grounds
where many untold stories await

when worlds gather at King's Square
marvel at the city market's iron
generations reverse like Wolastoq

even Houdini once spent the night
under twinkling lights illuminating
a port parade in transition

not knowing where we landed
we exchanged country names
for low and high tides

fog spirits bridge across Saint John
to many who call this old beginning
a new home

GOTHIC ARCHES

Citizens corner Wentworth Street to witness arches fall.

For those who need strength and beauty, a point where both sides press.

A developer bought the land, a stone church built in 1878, four seasons

after a not-so-great fire.

He plans to build apartments eight stories high to house empty-nesters.

Artists turn shards of stained glass into earrings.

Pigeons nest in what remains of the arcade.

Birds protest one last sunset in the rubble.

Oorhh! the pigeon remembers when Darwin joined London's pigeon clubs.

HOW THEORY WORKS

Theory is a process of shaming.   Theory is harmful.

Theory is hidden
in the story.

Theory is out of context.   Theory avoids emotions.

Theory injures.
Theory justifies.
Theory is a hammer.
Theory pushes back.
Theory dissects.
Theory creates jobs for critics.

Theory should speak to a larger audience.

Theory names.
Theory is dichotomy.
Theory opens.
Theory is praxis.
Theory is connective.

Theory needs to be accessible.

Theory pivots.
Theory questions.
Theory symbolizes.
Theory knows the code.
Theory situates.

Theory is concerned about the emotional labour of cats, how their purrs calm us.

Theory creates fields of study.
Theory brings pencils.
Theory is a science.
Theory is opera.
Theory blurs.
Theory is a missionary.

Theory is a kind of kinship.   Theory is inherently selective.

Theory responds.
Theory pluralizes.
Theory encodes.
Theory grew up in poverty.
Theory echoes patterns.
Theory needs to take ownership.

Theory needs to be responsible.   Theory isn't a church.

Theory cracks things open.
Theory blooms.
Theory ruptures.
Theory feminizes.
Theory cockblocks.
Theory has consequences.

Theory is finding validity.   Theory needs room for elasticity.

Theory puts things into boxes.
Theory intersects.
Theory is sexy.

Theory queers.
Theory measures.
Theory has no natural locus.

DEAR ELIZABETH BISHOP

I'm writing a book about the tides, and sipping a glass of Tidal Bay in a fish house in Lunenburg off Cornwallis. I've brought a small bottle of whisky for you, as I know it's your poison of choice. Would you like two fingers or four?

Listen—in "The Map," you reference the *shadow of Newfoundland*, and moreover *Labrador's yellow*, calling Inuit peoples moony Eskimos. We don't use that word anymore—it's derogatory. Also, have you ever been to Labrador? I don't think it's yellow. You published this poem in *North & South* in 1946, three years before Confederation, when Newfoundland joined the so-called nation. The collection won the Pulitzer Prize, Elizabeth. No small feat.

You died at 68 years of age in 1979. A cerebral aneurysm in your Boston apartment.

You had eight more years than my mother, but after your father died when you were months old, your mother lost the plot.

No wonder poets lose themselves in their cups. Life is too close to earth's surface.

Why am I writing to you now, in a body beyond your orbit? I guess because I wish you were here with me sitting at this old wooden table, one year into a global pandemic, something I swore I wouldn't write about, but here we are. A virus erupted, rearranged all our lives.

The *art of losing*? We're learning to master it. You're right—it's a disaster.

I am back in Nova Scotia—my architect lost his job and we had to move. Can I ask you about Lota? Do you see a correlation between architecture and poetry? Architects and poets speak in abstracts and space, small and large gestures. You said Brazil had *too many waterfalls*. We spent most of our days in New Brunswick chasing falling water.

Over a decade ago I visited your grandparents' house in Great Village, where you summered as a girl. Petit-Louis. Vil de Cadets. A village of Acadians, built on dykes in the salt marshes. We sat by *Sestina's* stove. *Reading the jokes from the almanac.* I slept in your childhood room. I never missed my girlhood room until my mother died, and her ex-lover dragged up a greedy lawsuit.

Now I miss crayons, teakettle, and tears.

Would you like another drink? I want to keep this strange dream going. I'll fix us blood orange bourbons. Let's go sip them with the map-makers and sing out to a seashore town.

I am trying not to get too lost at the seaweeded ledges, Elizabeth. But I am leaning over *to lift the sea from under.* I can't see Ursa Major, but Google just messaged me to say include: 7 countries, 246 cites, and 1,757 places. Tell me *what is a map?* What do you see, Greater She-Bear?

YOU CAME BACK ON FULL MOON

driving along the highway
with a trunk full of crinoline
your heart in fourth gear
roadside signs feverish

I wait beneath grandmother's glow,
where a jazz bar swings around the corner,
scoring the soundtrack of who we were,
where we've been, and what notes we'll hit

MAGNETIC MORTAL TRIP

modern medicine transforms
but couldn't save my mother
her new liver occupied
the cancer a receding glacier

I want to spiral with her
ice arriving over centuries
unfolding into cosmic hearsay

HOLDING HANDS DOWN AMELIA STREET

My moods are inversely related to the clarity of the sky.
—Glenn Gould

two lovers stunned by blooming wisteria,
one talks to the cows at Riverdale Zoo,
the other points towards Edwardian details

a blundering mind lost the car,
only to find another side of the city,
drinking at the only bar around
serving Fogo Island croquettes

walking off cheap whisky on rain-slick sidewalks,
circling fragments of childhood, they moved closer together
on a damp promenade, only stopped to bend
and kiss in Glenn Gould's garden

MIDSUMMER SPIRALLING A LABYRINTH

A labyrinth is a symbolic journey ...
but it is a map we can really walk on,
blurring the difference between map and world.
                              —Rebecca Solnit

in a garden of tangles
overlooking Grand Pré
my lover follows my footsteps
we ask ourselves—
what do we need to know at this time?

neither of us remember the way in
or know the way out
we seek clarity in ancient spirals
a geometry to release tidal tensions
open to all things nonrational

you can get lost in the morass
when the moon is tired
seeking the ephemeral
we enter intuitive realms
pilgrimage the symbolic openings

in the sacred circle of hearth
lavender blooms in our bloodstream
sprites drift through star formations
ratios tune like musical instruments
waves call us to the centre

a wavelength is not a maze
or the suspension of truth
making confessions in an herb garden
we meet again at the circle sculpture
lock eyes, and walk back aligned

MOONSTRUCK

I'm like the wind
made of grandmothers and moonstone
I dream in the seventh crown
the blue-white sheen of feldspar
lovers put lunar stones on their lips
when the moon is full to see a future

if we ever marry, will you give me moonstone?
could you pop it right in my mouth—
to kiss-off other dimensions?
or shall we go deep, spiral inward
and cycle life?

tides become moonstruck
at the pull and release of rhythm
we will face strange animal behaviours
when energy grows and power wanes

your grandmothers, my grandmothers,
guides who nurture us both rail us into action
calling me down to the dirt
shifting us towards seedlings
in honour of their deep feminine
they bring us earthbound to season

WANING GIBBOUS

COSMOLOGY OF ROUGH MAGIC

look up ways to work with the moon's stoicism
what phase it was the day you were born
tides and emotions marking orbits

observe each cycle's passing
first quarter burn your associations
last quarter shed what was never yours

search the sky without shame
quickfire energy ebbs
forget what you cannot grow

LEMON CAME IN THE NIGHT

dreaming in a borrowed bed
a woman made of primary colours
woke me like a victory undeclared

she led me to a garden, squeezed lemon juice
all over my body, sticking rinds in my mouths
told me to suck it all in—
my girl, you are citrus

NOT KNOWING THE BOOK OF MYTHS

we are not garbage
wearing the body armour of glitter

we share stories
need bodies
to know belonging

we sing songs
to carry on
we don't kneel
to make an altar
we believe in realms
of one another

there is light in this gutter
here, we are the stars
make room for something larger

we are facts and figures
order in the universe
chaotic rags of divinity
creators of our kind

from macrocosms
a body and mind
roots and constellations
linked to parts unknown

earth, air, fire, water
we are bone breath

YOU CAN'T FLY ON ONE WING

equal parts of all that we have not said
uncorking what we cannot know
let bubbles from the earth reveal
our ounces exposed

SLOW DANCING IN A BACHELOR APARTMENT TO JONI MITCHELL

the needle hits a groove
we become clouds
sway before sky
pulling each other close
never wanting to be blue again

MOTHER'S RUIN

gin wasn't my mother's ruin
she drank Black Tower with ice
a glass or two before she let go

once married to an alky
didn't think wine earned its keep
she knew the cost

when I started sipping as a teenager
she poured all her liquor down the drain

I kept drinking anyway—
found a kind of medicine
never realizing it was cancerous

EROTIC ECOLOGY

this burning ignites matter
erotic ecology is intimate
too personal to write about

why is it so hard to write about love

SOBER MOON

if the moon's wobbling
lowering water at low tide
later pushing tides higher
where we will be in ten years

no one owns the ocean floor
or controls lunar node cycles
we're reading horoscopes like omens
texting our way to the moon

praying it's just a tide-raising phase
bypassing gravitational pulls,
a façade of sea levels rising
while the flooding moon wobbles

LAST QUARTER

PUSH / PULL

in order to survive this polarizing year
I became copper, softened,
fleshy pinkish-orange unearthed

something inside turns malleable
here's the thing about vulnerability:
there are no denying instincts

RETURNING CLOSER TO EARTH TIME

on a canoe trip between Azure
and Dividing Lakes, only the waters know
I fear cancer, *ask* should I go?

it takes time to shed ourselves
remove another layer of decay
paddle in further, wave to wave

will I see what I'm being shown?
can I hear? will I even listen?
how do I hold an offering?

ego wants to play its own drama:
if I make her scared enough
she won't go

YOU WERE NEVER A VISITOR TO THIS WORLD

on your deathbed you wore lipstick
asked me to retrace your mouth
even though you could hardly speak

you wore vintage clip-on earrings
smiled a gap-toothed grin you once hid
a pink cashmere shawl around your shoulders

you didn't care for mint paper gowns
even dying you were all dolled up
you commanded the room

the nurse who shared your middle name
couldn't get over your steady gaze
the sea-grey blue of your eyes

when my father took the subway to hold
your hand for the first time in 35 years,
I saw something I never had before

he told a story of when a boy met a girl,
smashed together like bottles of pilsner
only with a hammer, shards of glass scattered over grass

until they lit the box of beer on fire
called himself a *bad actor, boozehound*
caught up in his character

in our last moments together
you called me over to your hospital bed whispered

tell your father it's time to go home

I NEED TO BE HELD BY SOMETHING OTHER THAN A THEORY

I don't want a theory; I want the poem inside me. I want the
poem to unfurl like a thousand monks chanting inside me.
—Sina Queyras

Grief refrains us. Words fail to contain it.

I am caught off guard by your last photograph. How it divides the present, and keels over.

Where is this place to hold, and be held by?

Try to read other poets, theorists, people. No one knows what to do, so they apologize.

Learn that loss has its own time, and you are a small animal reeling.

Swim in pools of Freud's theory, only to forget what I've read.

Write several elegies upside down.

Softly tell the body, this is only temporary.

WILD GEESE CAME

on the day you died
as winter moon rose
　　　the sky was cobalt blue

your body floated into sunrise
you didn't waste a day
you wrote lifetimes

I watched geese in open water
hover on the frozen St. Lawrence
wishing the Old World held
a few more like you

FINAL VIEW OF BELL ISLAND

Bell Measuring 9.7 kilometres in length and 3.5 kilometres in
width, Bell Island has an area of 34 square kilometres.

                                        —**Wikipedia**

when great-grandmother died,
my Nan threw herself over Ordovician
sandstone, shale, and red hematite

Mother never wanted to be buried,
so I scattered her ashes off flat rock
tossed orange roses into grey ocean
down the Irish shore

I nearly threw up Ediacaran fossils
a bodily reaction like my grandmother's,
arms stretched, falling forward,
please don't go without me

Mom asked me to put her ashes
under her saltbox
but I was told
no one wants your mother's
remains under their house

I put her name on a bench on Bell Island
to be placed across from Grandmother's grave,
mothers buried with their mothers,
but no room left for me—
the graveyard already too full

WANING CRESCENT

POEM FOR FRIDA KAHLO AS MOTHER

packing dollar store plastic flowers
to tie my hair in pink and yellow
marigolds to mirror your signature style
I call on you, call you *Mother*—
because I can't phone my own, she died.
you're dead, too, but your work sustains Mother Mexico
your monkeyed self-portraits offer multiple selves:
one subject—a fixed gaze, a steel brow
another self—orangey florals piled high
selves becoming morning glory,
Mexican chocolate, sunflower cosmos
almost good enough to eat.

SOLITUDE

She could be herself, by herself.
　　　—Virginia Woolf

Where are you now? Are you *in the little space of sky that sleeps next to the moon*? I'm not convinced of the lunar gateway. All my life, you were here, and now you've become sky? I don't buy it. I've studied the names of clouds—cumulus, cirrus, flammagenitus. If you were a cloud formation, you'd be firestorm. But you're not a cloud. I cannot imagine you are sleeping next to the moon. You never slept much, anyway. Have you become earth? I'm not sure that fits either. You never liked to walk barefoot in soil or sand. Not one for spending time outdoors. You obsessed over furniture; how empty chairs sat facing one another. Daily you plumped all the cushions. You said the neighbours made you anxious. The lack of trees made you feel seen. Things were calmer for you inside than out. You could control the temperature, the climate, the conversation. Now that you're no longer in your box house, I don't know where you are. Down the southern shore? Everyone is calling out in strange, clipped voices. Tiny human pleas, where is she? Maybe Grandmother knows where you are, but we don't know where she is either. Sometimes I find her in the line between horizon and sea. Other times chopping up onions, or peeling carrots. Some of us find pockets of her within ourselves. We're stuck here with the vegetable peels, *halfway to truth*. Are you *tangled in gold mesh*, or caught up in *the deceptiveness of beauty*? The so-called great beyond. You hated cooking, preferred restaurants and takeout. I bet nobody cooks where you are. You always said that you liked to be alone, that you could only be yourself, by yourself. Next to the ocean, nowhere else. You taught us not to become too attached. Now you've left us more alone than ever. Before you only shut the storm door, never locked it. Drew the curtains. Closed the blinds. You didn't care for daylight. Told us you needed a few moments alone in order to watch an hour of *the Young and the Restless*, and tune into yourself.

You once told me not all women are cut out for motherhood. Best choose your method wisely.

MOONSPELL: HOW TO MAKE MOONWATER

1. Eat up all the jam in the jar. Clean out the glassware.
2. Pour some water into the jar. Close it up tight.
3. Put your water jar on the windowsill on or near the full moon.
4. Find a moonpool to illuminate the water. Let your jar of water sit overnight.
5. Collect your moonwater at daybreak, no later than a moment past dawn.
6. Moonwater pairs well with mocktails, rituals, or summoning.
7. Use your moonwater sparingly.

TRAVEL LIGHT, MY LOVE

may silence be our splendour
may we get to know our old selves—
consider ourselves rising

HIGH TIDE

bulging like the earth and moon
we're at high tide, rearranging our bedroom
to fit equal parts, you plus me

I'VE BEEN TAKEN BY COLETTE

on her maiden voyage into Conception Bay
dangling our toes over the Atlantic
we blew kisses to sea beings

your moontime came
as I ovulated, and we got stranded
on the rocks between land and sea

fingering watery seagrass
combing a mermaid's hair off Kellys Island
surrounded by devil's fenceposts

your French beau in his off time
scaled the rocks in a wetsuit
to pick us the freshest chanterelles

beached on a boat named after Colette
we waited out low tide like my grandmother moons ago
to ring the bells off Bell Island

GROUNDWATER

you were leaving earth's mantle
your breath eroding
towards spirit world

you told the nurse—*I want*
to go home to Newfoundland,
having saved for new windows
in your old saltbox

I held your hand until I couldn't
tried to grasp the ocean floor
but grief's gravitas found me

rebounding towards sky
questioning the Ice Age
moving underground

one year later
memory fossilizes
throwing your ashes off the Drook

you broke off barren crust
recycled into groundwater
pushed up icebergs
flattened moonlight

we put down a concrete bench
facing your mother and grandmother
your place of rest not far from
where wild horses run

WILD(ISH)

anchored by land and water
this island's spell:

I want to be a seashell
I want to be a mold
I want to be a spirit

the only drink is:
wildness as tonic

HOMING

Mom used to go to the cove
stretch her arms out to the wind
look to the fog-capped sky
and deeply exhale: *I'm home*

Dad got on a ladder yesterday
first time since the stroke
said he: *took one step up*
saw the roof, and felt at home

I have to go far down swimming
under a boat moon to depths unknown
until my lungs almost burst
to find myself whole

LOOKING GLASS TIDES

an image evokes a sense of departure,

a release of energy through body

physical shifts in what it means to harbour

life's exhibition invites you to look through the binoculars

of your archival photographs

then asks you to shake off your ties

MOONLIGHT EPITAPH

I've never tried to write an epitaph to blue moonlight
but I had to describe our mother
our teacher
our rough ocean love
our beautiful wild
inscribed on rock
only left to wonder
did I get it right?
will anyone understand her path—
her light beam
my lunar gateway

since she left I'm seeing
her journey more clearly
the stress of being alive

THE LOSING OF THE MOON

I fall asleep to she-moon over Pier 28
where a tower churns bushels of grist
wake to waning light above grain elevators
lowering my dreams into tides—
suddenly pregnant with lunar fight

night left me, like my mother at daybreak
when morning came I wondered
how had she become iridescence?
given we started out husking kernels
curbside many moons back

layers of deception re-story my origin
but can I ever know my source?
this body remembers my first ocean
rafts of maternal shoreline folded until
I hit a port, and decided to stay

NOTES ON THE POEMS

"Time: A Biography," and "Greater Than Average Tides," are published in the exhibition catalogue *Harbour: A Compendium*, curated by Amy Ash (Amy Ash Art & Engagement), June 2020.

"Ecology of Being" was written at the Banff Centre for the Arts in spring 2019 after a workshop with Liz Howard. The title inspired Duo Concertante's commissioning project of five new classical works, of which composer Melissa Hui's piece, *Ecology of Being* for violin, piano, and actor, features my poems "Ecology of Being" and "Sleeping with the Northern Lights." It was recorded by Duo Concertante at the Glenn Gould Studio in Toronto and will be released in 2022. The work was made into a film directed by Nicola Hawkins and won Best Experimental Short and Best Original Score at the Los Angeles 2020 IndieX Film Fest. It was also a semifinalist at the 2020 Montreal Independent Film Festival, was selected for the 2020 London Lift-Off Film Festival and the 2021 Unscripted Twillingate Digital Arts Festival, and nominated for the 2021 London Eco Film Festival.

"Ecology of Being," "Aurora Alert," and "If I Wasn't a Fury" are published in *QWERTY 41, The Ecology Issue*, Summer 2020.

"Home Was Calling" was written in response to "Wildness: An Ode to Newfoundland and Labrador" by Jeremy Charles.

"If I Wasn't a Fury," "I Am Pulsar," and "Not Knowing the Book of Myths" was written in residence at The Theatre Centre in Toronto as part of Stewart Legere's collaborative project, *The Unfamiliar Everything*. Rae Spoon and Legere have transformed "If I Wasn't a Fury" into melody, Winter 2018.

"Hinge" is a found poem from *Mrs. Dalloway* by Virginia Woolf, taken from *Selected Works of Virginia Woolf* (Ware, UK: Wordsworth Editions, 2005): 129–130.

"She Looks Straight Ahead" draws from Antônio Carlos Jobim's "The Girl from Ipanema" (recorded by João Gilberto and Stan Getz in 1964).

"Rooftop Oracles" is a found poem from my review "Postmodern Blackness in Heather Hart's Northern Oracle," published in *Visual Arts News*, Spring 2020.

"Kepe'kek / At the Narrows" was written in response to *Kepe'kek from the Narrows of the Great Harbour*, a collective youth-based photo project on exhibit at the Art Gallery of Nova Scotia that commemorated the Mi'kmaq community destroyed in the Halifax Explosion of 1917.

"Portals" is a found poem from my review "Art's Higher State: The Vision and Practice of Deanna Musgrave," published in *Created Here Magazine*, Issue 11, Spring 2020.

"Menagoesg Redux," was commissioned by the City of Saint John for its 235th birthday (237th Loyalist Day) and Victoria Day virtual celebrations during COVID-19, Spring 2020.

"Portals" and "How Theory Works" are published in *Marsh Blue Violet Queer Poetry from New Brunswick*, edited by RM Vaughan, with French translation by Sophie M. Lavoie, Frog Hollow Press, 2021.

"Dear Elizabeth Bishop" features lines from Elizabeth Bishop's poems "The Map," "One Art," "Sestina," published in *Elizabeth Bishop: The Complete Poems* 1927–1979, Farrar, Straus and Giroux, 1984.

"Solitude" borrows from *To the Lighthouse* by Virginia Woolf, (London: Hogarth Press, 1927): pages 48 and 60.

"WILD(ISH)" features the lines "I want to be a seashell. I want to be a mold. I want to be a spirit." These are the opening lines of Noboru Kawazoe's Metabolist manifesto in architecture, from the conceptual manifesto *Metabolism 1960: Proposals for a New Urbanism*. It's also the title of Lou Sheppard and William Robinson's Fall 2021 exhibition at the Dalhousie Art Gallery.

"Looking Glass Tides" is a found poem from my review of "Harbour," an exhibition curated at the Beaverbrook Gallery by Amy Ash, published in *Visual Arts News*, Summer 2020.

The title "Moonlight Epitaph" was inspired by "Epitaph for Moonlight," the title of choral music by R. Murray Schafer from *A Garden of Bells: Choral Music of R. Murray Schafer, Vol. 1*, recorded by the Vancouver Chamber Choir in 1986.

"The Losing of the Moon" comes from a chapter title in Michael Crummey's *River Thieves*, published by Anchor Canada, 2001.

ACKNOWLEDGEMENTS

Deepest thanks to Jay and Hazel Millar, my co-publishers, who continue to support my poetic journey. As well as my editor Jónína Kirton, who crystalized this book into its final lunar phase. A special thanks to Amy Ash, for her stunning cover artwork, Shannon Whibbs for her attentive copy editing, and Tree Abraham for the book's design.

This collection was written over many moon cycles to honour my late mother, Diane Campbell, who remains my eternal light. As well as for my father, Kevin Webb, from whom my stubborn and fierce poetic sense stems. I would like to extend my love to my grandmothers and grandfathers, Robert Beattie (Poppy) and the late Amelia Beattie (Nanny), as well as the late Mary, Doris, and Aiden Webb.

This book is also for my brother, James Campbell, and his daughter, Celia Anne Amelia Campbell, whom Nana loved beyond words. For my spirited and beautiful aunts: Veralynn and Wendy Beattie. Also, to my sister-cousin Ice Tha One/Angela Musceo, Jordon Musceo, Wesley, and Jack Rising.

Also, I extend my sincere gratitude to Graham Campbell and Mary Jean Clark-Campbell, my sisters, brothers, and all my nieces and nephews. As well as to the Gray family, who have warmly welcomed me into their hearts.

I would like thank Stuart Everitt and Hilary Dennis whose love carries. Also, to Tracy O'Brien, Deanna Musgrave, Virginia Woolf, Grandview Street North, Lindsay Shane, Cherie Dimaline, Lunenburg, Shannon Pringle, Portugal Cove South, Amelia Reimer, Lucas Crawford, Heather Jessup, Anna Swanson, Ashley Gwyneth Imonetti, Alex Ash, Lou Sheppard, Laurier Avenue, RM Vaughan, Kelly S. Thompson, Stewart Legere, North River, Frida Kahlo, Monica Walsh, Lee Maracle, Kim Harris, Nancy Harn, Linda Morra, Charlotte Street, Bell Island, Sabine LeBel, Cassidy McFadzean, Germain Street, Colette, the Drook, The Tangled Garden, shalan joudry, Guylaine Williams, Tanya Evanson, Bagno a Ripoli, Elizabeth Bishop, Liz

Howard, the team at *Visual Arts News*, Jocelyn Parr, Inglis Street, Erin Wunker, Tanya Davis, Vicky Chainey Gagnon, Bart Vatour, Rachel McCrum, the Princess Margaret Cancer Centre, Amelia Street, Virginia Trieloff, the cod, and the many artists, poets, and places who inspire shifts.

Much gratitude to Sue Sinclair, Jennifer Andrews, and my committee at University of New Brunswick, as well as Douglas Walbourne-Gough, Thom Vernon, and Triny Finlay. I appreciate the support of the Banff Centre of the Arts, the Canada Council for the Arts, as well as the opportunity to have my poetry transformed into classical music by Nancy Dahn and Timothy Steeves of Duo Concertante, Clara Steeves, and composer Melissa Hui.

Finally, to my love Andrew Gray, for whom *Lunar Tides* also charts the ebb and flow of our tidal rhythms. Wela'lin for riding out the waves, and for slowly swaying with me at the full and change of the moon.

ABOUT THE AUTHOR

© Meghan Tansey Whitton

Shannon Webb-Campbell is a mixed Indigenous (Mi'kmaq) settler poet, writer, and critic. She is the author of *Still No Word* (2015), recipient of Eagle Canada's Out in Print Award, and *I Am a Body of Land* (2019; finalist for the A.M. Klein Prize for Poetry). Shannon holds an MFA in Creative Writing from the University of British Columbia, and a MA in English Literature at Memorial University of Newfoundland and Labrador, and is a doctoral candidate at the University of New Brunswick in the Department of English. She is the editor of *Visual Arts News Magazine*. Shannon is a member of Qalipu Mi'kmaq First Nation and lives in Kijpuktuk / Halifax in Mi'kma'ki.

COLOPHON

Manufactured as the first edition of
Lunar Tides
in the spring of 2022 by Book*hug Press

Edited for the press by Jónína Kirton
Copy edited by Shannon Whibbs
Proofread by Rachel Gerry
Type + design by Tree Abraham

Printed in Canada

bookhugpress.ca